Discovering KNIGHTS and CASTLES

Richard Platt

Illustrations by Inklink

ReD KiTE

First published in the UK in 2003 by Red Kite Books,
an imprint of Haldane Mason Ltd
PO Box 34196, London NW10 3YB
info@haldanemason.com

Copyright © Haldane Mason Ltd, 2003

ISBN 1-902463-63-3 (with banner)
ISBN 1-902463-64-1 (without banner)

A HALDANE MASON BOOK
Art Director : Ron Samuel
All original artwork : Inklink, Firenze, Italy
The picture on page 19 (top) is reproduced by courtesy of the author

Colour reproduction by One Thirteen Ltd, UK

Printed in China

Contents

Building Castles

Medieval castles grew out of simple enclosures behind deep ditches or high earth banks into great stone fortresses with forbidding walls protecting a central keep. Their purpose was simple: to keep those inside safe from their enemies outside.

The first castles were hardly more than circular hill-top mounds of earth, surrounded by deep trenches. But these simple earth ramparts were enough to protect the people inside from attack by their warrior neighbours. Capturing them wasn't easy: attackers had to fight their way uphill from the foot of the trench to the top of the circular ridge.

The castles that followed had wooden walls on top of their earthen embankments. These walls gave the castles extra strength and height, so that defenders

▲ **The first castles:** simple earth castles may be as much as 7,000 years old, but traces of them can still be seen in many places throughout Europe.

had a commanding view and stronger protection against their foes.

The Norman people of France combined earth and timber in their motte-and-bailey castles. The strong wooden fortresses sat at the top of a motte or mound. At the foot of the mound, the bailey was a courtyard protected by a simple timber fence or palisade. People from outside the castle retreated into the large open courtyard with their farm animals when danger threatened.

▸ **Motte-and-bailey castles:** these were built by the Norman people of northern France in the 10th and 11th centuries.

Timber castles had one crucial weakness: they could be burned down. Replacing the wooden stockade at the top of the motte with a stone keep made it fire-proof. Keep-building began around the 12th century. However, stone castles were not an entirely new invention then. More than a thousand years earlier, the soldiers of the powerful Roman empire had built stone castles. They used them to guard the land they conquered as they spread out from their native Italy. Earlier still, the empires of Egypt, Greece and Mesopotamia had protected their cities with stone and mud-brick walls.

In the Middle Ages (the period of history that began when the Roman empire crumbled in 476 AD), stone-built keeps were used by wealthy and powerful lords as bases from which to control the surrounding land. As time passed, the lords added extra defences, including stone-walled baileys, watch-towers at the corners, reinforced gatehouses, and ditches or water-filled moats. By the 15th century, European castles had become hard to improve any more. Rings of strong walls surrounded the keep, which was so strong that it was almost impossible to capture by force.

▴ **The keep:** defenders retreated to the safety of the keep when an attacking army captured the castle's outer walls.

Castle-building came to an end around 1500. The power of kings and queens had grown. Warlords and barons, who had been the main builders of castles, were less important – and less wealthy – than they had once been. Around the same time, a new weapon, the cannon, was changing the way in which wars were fought. The cannon balls it fired could blast a hole in even the thickest castle wall.

Castles didn't disappear altogether – today's nuclear shelters, buried deep underground, serve the same purpose as the castles of the Middle Ages.

◂ **High walls:** together with deep ditches, these guard the 12th-century castle of Haut Königsburg in Alsace, France.

'Who's there?' The guard calls from the castle,
   And then he hears the faint reply –
A voice no louder than a field mouse:
   'Help me, please, or I will die!
My father was a noble knight
   Struck down in battle by a sword.'
The guards have pity on the orphan
   And take him in to see their lord.

Training to be a Knight

There was more to becoming a knight than just buying a suit of armour and a horse. Knighthood was not just a special kind of armoured warfare. It was a whole way of life, with its own code of honour, called chivalry.

The life of a knight in the Middle Ages was very different from that of a soldier today. A knight fought out of honour and duty. In exchange for joining the army of a powerful lord, a knight received land to farm and perhaps a house to live in. His master, in turn, had duties and rewards. His duty was to raise an army of knights to fight for a still more powerful lord, or for the king or queen. His reward – like the knight's – was land, and power over his subjects: the people who lived on it.

The process of becoming a knight wasn't quick or easy. For a start, you had to be a boy, and you had to have the right parents. All knights were from noble families – rich and powerful

▲ **Growing up:** until the age of seven, children had no real education. Even in their games, though, boys copied the skills of knights.

people who were the highest class of people in society at that time.

Noble parents sent their sons away from home as soon as they were seven years old. The boys went to live in the homes of other noble families, where they studied and worked as pages. Becoming a page was the first step in training to be a knight.

In his new home, a page was usually taught by a chaplain (a priest). He learned reading and writing – in English, French, and Latin – and studied the Bible and arithmetic. He was taught to ride a horse, and to hunt with dogs and falcons. He learned how to be a gentleman, how to behave correctly, and what it meant to be a knight.

At the age of 14, a page who had mastered all these skills became a squire. He continued

Hawking and Hunting

Today, hunting and falconry are often thought of as cruel sports, but in the Middle Ages they were an important part of a squire's training. No knight could call himself a gentleman unless he could tell the difference between a peregrine falcon and a sparrow-hawk – two of the birds of prey that were trained to swoop on hares, rabbits or smaller birds. Traditionally, squires trained falcons called lanner falcons, slowly taming them by feeding them morsels of meat and stroking them with a feather or bird's wing. Once trained, a bird would be its owner's constant companion. Though it had complete freedom when hunting, the hawk or falcon would always return when called with a whistle.

Hunting with hounds was perhaps more difficult for a squire to master. Adult hunters followed the dogs at a gallop, and boys on smaller, slower horses often got left behind. There was more to learn, too, with each animal hunted only at certain seasons, and correct and proper rituals to follow at each stage of the hunt.

▸ **Hawking:** only noble men were allowed to hunt in the forests with dogs and hawks. Ordinary people caught taking game (hunt animals) risked severe punishment.

his education, served at meals, and helped a knight to put on armour and prepare for battle. A squire's serious training as a soldier began, too: he learned to fight with a sword and a lance.

The final step came at the age of 21, when a squire who had performed well and studied hard (and who could afford the enormous cost of armour, horses, and servants) was made a knight at a special ceremony. This began with prayer and other religious rituals. It ended when the squire's lord dubbed him – struck him a mock blow with a hand or a sword. The squire had become a knight at last.

Knights were expected to obey a code of behaviour called chivalry. They had to be brave, honest, gentle, truthful, religious, and loyal. They had to treat other people with respect – but this usually only applied to people who were equally noble. The code of chivalry did not always extend to ordinary people. Knights often treated people of lower rank badly, stealing their land, their food, and their possessions without a moment's thought.

The orphan's father was a knight,
  So he would like to be one too.
The Baron says, 'You'll be my page,
  And bow and scrape and kiss my shoe.'
As he grows up he learns the ropes
  And works his way up from the mire.
At fourteen years he's big and strong
  The Baron says, 'You'll be my squire.'

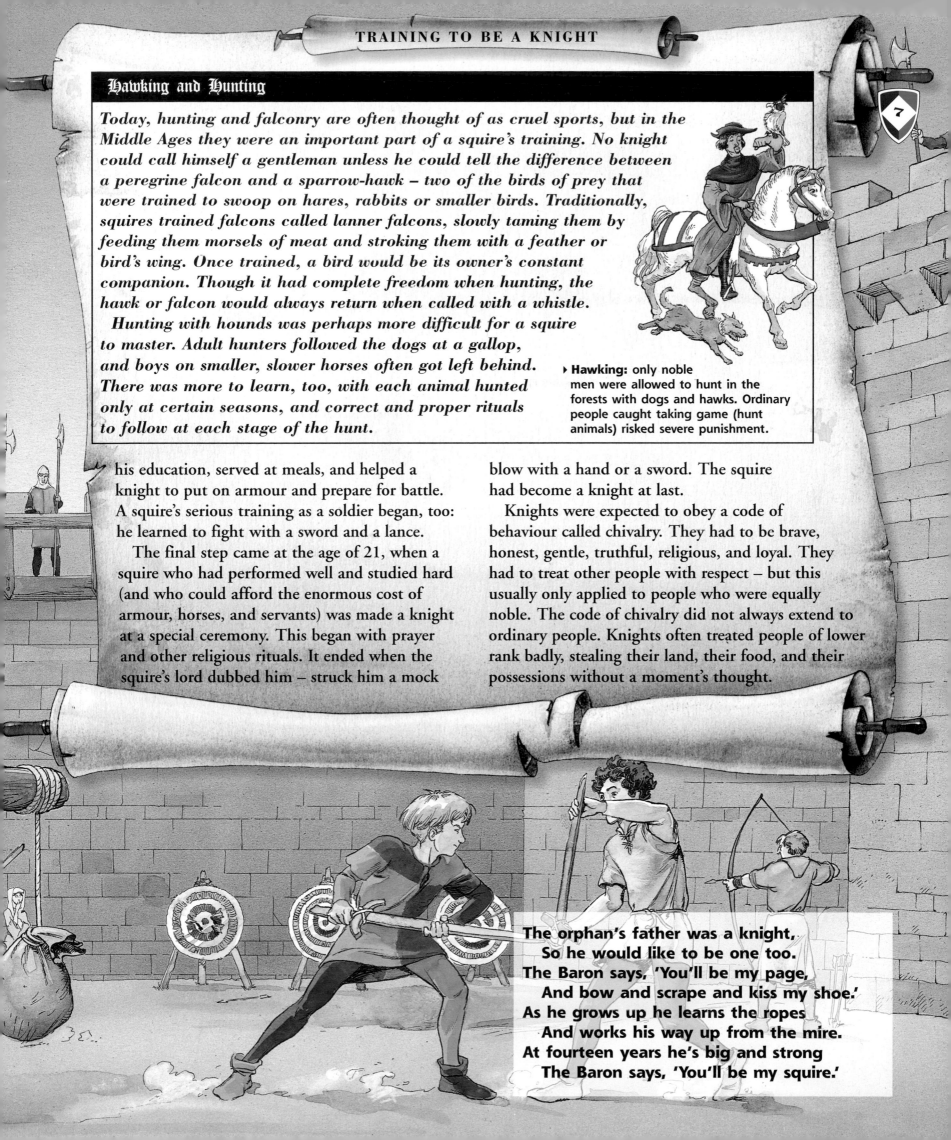

8

Everyday Life

As well as being a strong fortress, a castle was also a home and workplace to many people, from the lord and his family to the humblest soldier and servant. As a result, it was like a small town, full of bustling life.

A castle was a safe and secure refuge from attack in times of war and unrest. Wars were common in the Middle Ages, but there were also many peaceful times. Sometimes there was no fighting for years on end. In these calmer times, castles were still important. They provided homes for noble families and the people who worked in the castle.

In the keep at the very centre of the castle was the great hall. Banquets were held here, and daily meals, too, all prepared from the produce of the manor. This was the farmland and forest that surrounded

▲ **The forge:** a huge bellows pumped air into the forge's fire until the fire was hot enough to soften steel. Smiths then wielded heavy hammers to pound and shape the hot metal.

the castle, and provided much of its wealth (see pages 16–17). All the food was prepared in nearby kitchens, where cooks and their assistants laboured before great roaring fires (see pages 10–11).

Close to the hall were other household rooms, including the solar. At night this grand and comfortable room was the bedchamber for the lord and lady of the castle. During the day it served as an office and snug sitting-room for the family. Conveniently near the solar and hall were much smaller rooms for the dozens of servants who waited on the lord and his

As years go by he settles in,
   Becomes the family's favourite lad.
The Baron tells him while they're hunting:
   'You're like the son I never had.'
Then one day a coach arrives
   Bringing back the Baron's daughter.
The lovely maid's been long away –
   Our hero now resolves to court her.

family. The priest or chaplain had rooms here too. He needed to be close to his work, leading worship in the chapel, and teaching the castle children (see pages 6–7).

Farther away within the bailey, more buildings supplied the castle's needs. The stables took care of the horses used by the garrison (the castle guard) and also many more horses used for sport and enjoyment. Hunting and riding were popular, and wealthy people kept many horses for these pastimes. Hunting needed dogs, too, for chasing deer and hares, so near to the stable there was a kennel full of baying hounds.

The craftspeople who had workshops in the bailey included many whose trades were connected with riding and hunting. The forge was here, where blacksmiths shoed horses and made or repaired iron and bronze items. Leather workers cut and sewed saddles and bridles. Other craftspeople kept the fighting equipment of the castle ready for action. Workers in the armoury made and sharpened swords and other

▲ **A windmill:** circular stones inside a mill ground the grain into flour. It took a lot of power to turn the heavy millstones. This came from wind turning the mill's big sails. Mills could also be driven by water turning a water-wheel.

weapons, and created the metal plates and mail suits (see pages 22–3) that protected knights in battle.

Much of the bustling activity that took place inside the bailey was concerned with crops and food animals. The grain stores were here, and there might even be a windmill on the walls to grind the grain to flour for baking. In autumn, the bailey ran red with blood as farm animals were slaughtered and butchered, and their meat preserved either by smoking or by salting.

Even in peacetime, the castle needed some protection and policing. The garrison of knights and lesser soldiers who provided it usually lived in the towers. The gatehouse was their headquarters and weapons store. Captives and villains were locked – and forgotten – in the dungeon, the castle's underground prison.

Food and Cooking

A castle feast was a delight for the senses. While acrobats, musicians, and jugglers amused them, the diners at the long tables feasted on highly-spiced meat, fish, pies, and sugar sculptures, washing down their enormous meal with wine and strong ale.

The hungry guests who sat down at banquets in a castle's great hall had plenty of food to choose from. Wealthy people took pride in both the variety and the number of dishes they served at great feasts. As well as the roast meats we eat today, castle cooks served much less familiar dishes, such as swan, crane, heron, larks, and finches. From the sea they ate seals, porpoises, and whales as well as more usual fish.

It could be quite hard to taste or even recognize these different foods sometimes. Medieval cooks often dressed up dishes, disguising one kind of food as another, or combining foods in surprising ways. One recipe instructed the cook to sew the back of a piglet to the front of a large chicken; another called

▲ **The kitchen:** to supply a banquet, castle cooks butchered whole flocks of chickens, ducks, and geese. The kitchen also baked bread once or twice a week.

for cocks' combs and feet to be tossed in a salad. Cooks also mixed ingredients, combining fruit and meat, or sweet and sour flavours, similar to Eastern food today. Spices were used a lot, to disguise the taste of food and even to change the flavours altogether.

In creating their dishes, castle cooks faced some special challenges modern chefs don't share. Food had to be made so that it could be eaten with fingers because table settings did not include forks. Meat was roast and cut up before serving, or baked into pastry cases. Cooks ground up a lot of food into a paste. This made it easy to eat, especially for those people who had lost all their teeth.

Serving and eating these dishes was a grand ritual. A blast of trumpets announced the meal, then pages brought jugs of water and bowls so

Entertainment

At grand feasts, musicians and other entertainers amused the guests between courses. The minstrels were often travelling troubadours, who sang songs of love and chivalry. They also sang ballads about popular news topics of the day. In a world with no magazines or papers, their up-to-date songs brought welcome (and unwelcome) news. The songs entertainers sang were often vulgar, or performed in revealing costumes: 'The greater the feasts, the coarser were often the deeds and songs of the mirth-mongers.' Jugglers and acrobats also entertained the diners, throwing balls and clubs high in the air, and performing gravity-defying leaps and tumbles. Some medieval amusements we wouldn't find very amusing today. For example, performing animals, including dancing bears, were hugely popular. And people laughed at those with disabilities – jesters were often dwarfs or hunchbacks, or people suffering from mental illnesses.

▲ **Musicians:** minstrels were often well dressed, because they were paid in cloth or in the cast-off clothes of rich audiences. England's King Edward II (1284–1327) paid four minstrels 23 m/75 ft of cloth.

that guests could wash their hands. Diners put their food not on a plate, but on a trencher – a thick slice of stale bread. At the end of the meal, servants gave the gravy-soaked trenchers to the poor and hungry begging outside the castle wall.

Between courses, the kitchen produced more delicious treats, again heavily disguised. Subtleties were popular in the grandest households. Made from almond paste and costly sugar, subtleties were edible sculptures of subjects such as hunting scenes, mythical beasts, or ships in stormy seas.

▲ **Plain food:** the peasants who put fine food on the castle table themselves ate simpler dishes.

Though this luxury food was common on castle tables, ordinary people ate much plainer dishes. Most lived on a diet of bread, and beans flavoured with onions and garlic. They grew vegetables in their gardens, and meat or fish were treats. To get the energy needed for hard farm work, people drank ale (beer made without the bitter hop plant). Adults drank ale as alcoholic as today's strongest beer. Children drank 'single ale' which was less strong, but still alcoholic.

The larks and blackbirds have been silenced,
    The sucking pig no longer squeals.
They're killed and cooked and on the table
    With honeyed sweets and jellied eels.
The banquet's served and, as a squire,
    The boy serves wine to every guest.
While waiting on the Baron's daughter,
    He pours red wine down her new dress.

Castle People

A castle was a busy place. Servants and soldiers bustled everywhere, working to keep the castle safe, supplied, and running smoothly. Some wore colourful uniforms. A few dressed in elegant clothes. But hardly any of these workers were women.

A castle was a man's world. There were few women or girls among the servants and other workers who hurried to obey the commands of the lord and his family. Most of the female workers did jobs reserved for women in the world outside the castle walls. For example, women did the castle laundry, and they also brewed the ale. There was one job that no man could do: the wet-nurse breast-fed the babies of the lady of the castle.

Most female staff within the castle worked as personal servants and companions to the noble family. They helped the women and girls to dress and bathe, and kept them company.

▲ **Steward (left) and chamberlain (right):** together, these two ran the castle, taking care of all important decisions while the lord was away.

Almost members of the family, these lucky women received the cast-off clothes of their employers, so that it was sometimes hard to tell mistress and servant apart. In the same way, the men of the castle had close personal servants who dressed in their masters' old clothes and listened to their chatter.

There were very few of these plain-clothes personal servants. Far more of the castle staff wore the livery, or uniform, of their master. The most important of these was the steward, who was in charge of all the other household staff. He also made sure that the castle ran smoothly, taking charge of everything except

Boy and girl sit in the courtyard
And he plays a lovelorn tune.
Servants spot them in the shadows
And start to gossip: 'Marriage soon!'
Who's that, lurking in the corner,
Watching them, just like a sleuth?
It's a rival for her kisses,
A haughty, naughty, knavish youth.

military (fighting) matters. Almost as important, the chamberlain kept control of the great hall and the solar – the lord's bedchamber (see page 8).

Most of the other liveried servants were concerned with food and cooking. Besides the cook himself, the pantler was in charge of the pantry. The butler (bottler) looked after the barrels of wine and beer and filled bottles and jugs for the table. These servants were themselves quite important figures in the castle – important enough to have servants of their own. Indeed, in a big castle with a large staff, even the servant's servants had servants!

Not all of these lesser staff wore livery, unless they worked for the king or in the grandest households. Instead, their clothing revealed their trade. The turnspit, for example, roasted meat at the kitchen fire, and his work made his ragged

clothes greasy. The baker's lad would be dusty with flour. The tradesmen who worked in the bailey were as easy to recognize – such as the smith by his strong arms and leather apron, and the kennel lad by his filthy clothes that smelled of hounds.

A castle would not be a castle without its garrison (guard) of fighting men. Their commander, the constable, took charge of the defence of the castle when the lord was away – or he shared control with the lady. The rest of the time, the constable and the marshall, his second-in-command, organized the knights whose duty it was to keep the castle safe. In turn, the knights commanded the castle guard of archers and foot-soldiers who patrolled the walls and kept watch from the high towers.

◄ **Pantler (left) and butler (right):** the panter or pantler's name comes from the French word for bread – pain – because he was originally the castle baker. The butler's job was to serve wine at the table. He had assistants to do the hard work of bottling that gave his job its title.

◄ **Blacksmith (left), seamstress (right), and laundress (centre):** armourers, washerwomen, seamstresses and many other tradespeople worked within the castle walls, or just outside. A large castle might provide work for hundreds of skilled craftsmen and women, and as many labourers.

14

Health and Sanitation

Castles were not very healthy places. Dirty water, bad diet, diseases, and injuries all made people ill. Doctors did their best to cure the sick, but without modern drugs or scientific knowledge, they often did more harm than good.

The best way to recover from illness in the Middle Ages was not to get sick in the first place! Unfortunately, this wasn't easy. Some people died from accidents and injuries, but many died of diseases that can be cured today, such as measles, polio, and smallpox.

One of the most serious causes of disease was dirty water. Today, we know the importance of keeping water clean, but this wasn't always understood. Castle water came from wells, rivers and streams that were often polluted. Sometimes the castle lavatories themselves were the source of pollution.

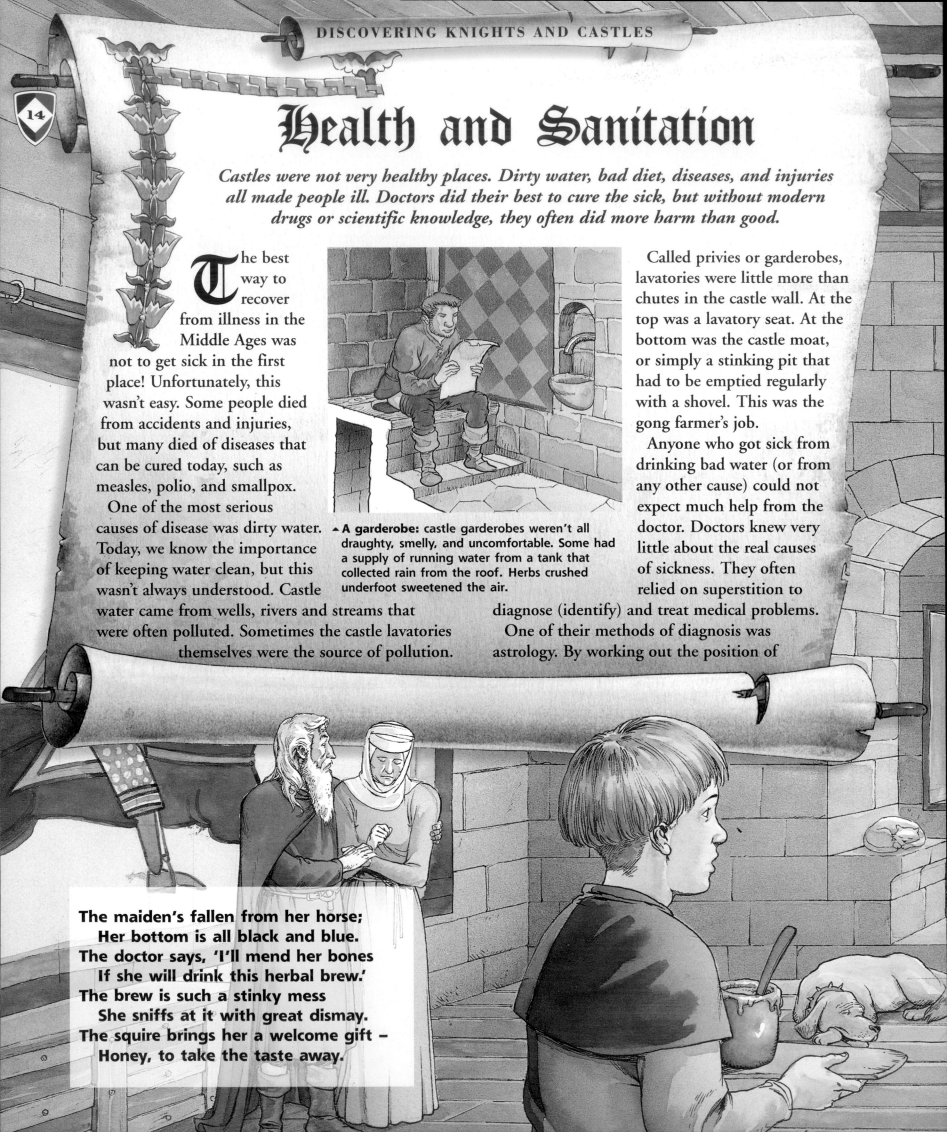

▲ **A garderobe:** castle garderobes weren't all draughty, smelly, and uncomfortable. Some had a supply of running water from a tank that collected rain from the roof. Herbs crushed underfoot sweetened the air.

Called privies or garderobes, lavatories were little more than chutes in the castle wall. At the top was a lavatory seat. At the bottom was the castle moat, or simply a stinking pit that had to be emptied regularly with a shovel. This was the gong farmer's job.

Anyone who got sick from drinking bad water (or from any other cause) could not expect much help from the doctor. Doctors knew very little about the real causes of sickness. They often relied on superstition to diagnose (identify) and treat medical problems. One of their methods of diagnosis was astrology. By working out the position of

The maiden's fallen from her horse;
    Her bottom is all black and blue.
The doctor says, 'I'll mend her bones
    If she will drink this herbal brew.'
The brew is such a stinky mess
    She sniffs at it with great dismay.
The squire brings her a welcome gift –
    Honey, to take the taste away.

the planets at the time of their patient's birth, they believed (wrongly) that they could find out the cause of the illness. Doctors also tried numerology – they gave a number to each letter of the patient's name and added them to find a cure.

One medieval method at least seems similar to something doctors do today, and that was to examine their patient's urine. Unfortunately, the lack of medical science at the time prevented the doctors from learning anything useful from it.

Once a doctor had decided what was wrong with a patient, he used similar methods to choose a cure. There was not a very wide choice. Herbal cures (see below) helped, but more often doctors prescribed blood-letting. They cut open the patient's vein with a sharp knife, and let blood flow out into a bowl. Exactly when the blood-letting took place was important,

▶ **Blood-letting:** although a popular practice in medieval times, blood-letting in fact weakens the body and hastens death. Far from draining blood away, modern doctors put fresh blood back into sick patients in blood transfusions.

◀ **Astrology:** medieval doctors relied on methods like astrology for cures, studying zodiac diagrams like this one.

and astrology and numerology were used to decide this. Blood-letting did not help patients to recover, however, and very often actually made them worse. Other popular remedies were fasting (not eating) and prayer. Fasting was as harmful in many cases as blood-letting.

Only wealthy people could afford to employ doctors. The poor cured themselves, and often did a better job of it. They just waited for nature to heal them, or relied on herbal remedies. Traditional healers – often wise old women – collected and prepared these remedies. Though many herbal cures did as little good as a castle doctor's numerology, some worked, and are still in use today. For example, willow bark, a traditional pain killer in medieval times, contains salicylic acid. Today we use aspirin, which contains the same chemical in a purer form.

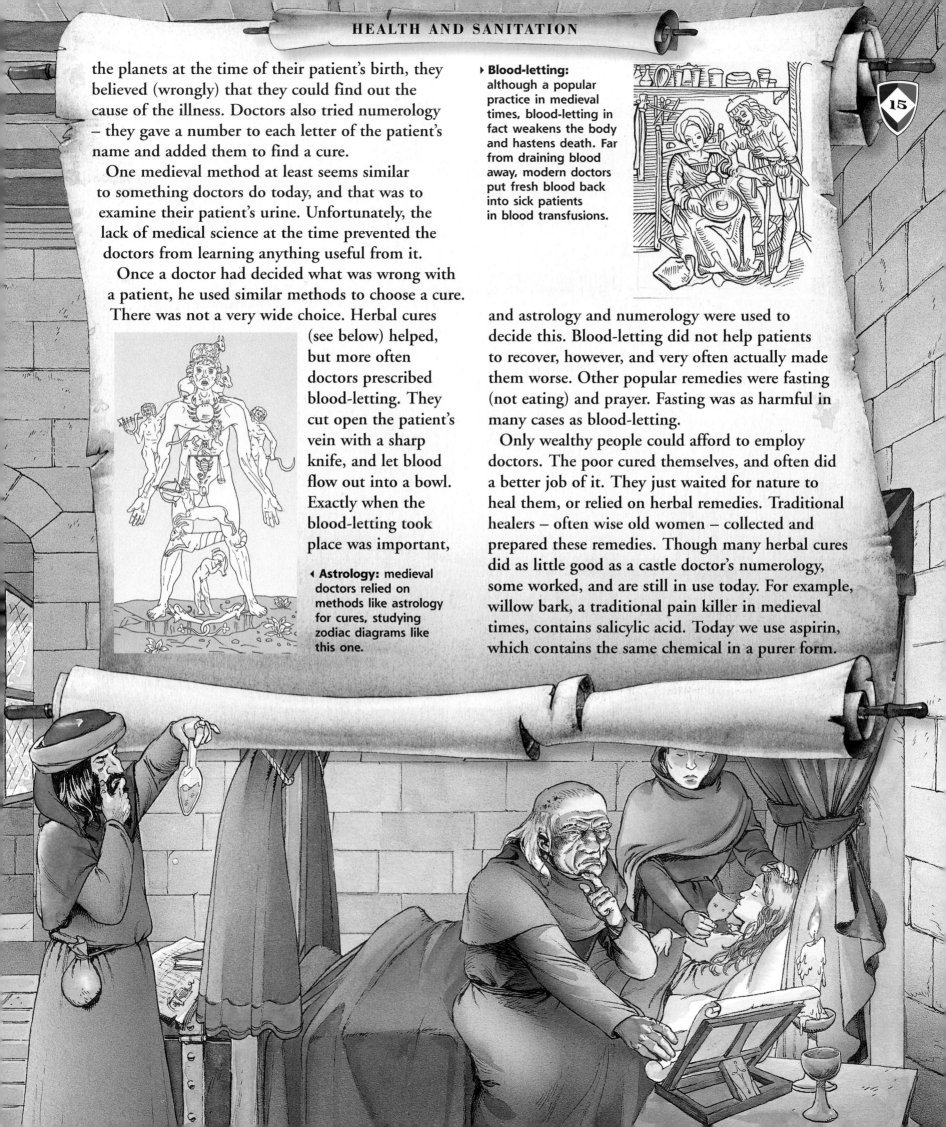

Castle and Manor

The lands outside the castle provided the food that was eaten inside. In summer, wheat and barley fields spread out from the walls like a golden carpet. The grain they produced made coarse bread and strong ale.

From the highest watch-tower of a castle, a sentry might look out over forests swarming with game, common land where animals grazed, and waving fields of grain. From all these places came food to feed the many hungry folk who gathered daily for meals in the castle's great hall.

The wildlife in European forests was a source of both food and sport, but hunting it was a privilege reserved for the lord of the manor. Ordinary people – peasants – caught trapping or stalking the deer, boar (wild pigs), and even rabbits and pigeons, faced severe punishment, such as blinding. What little meat these people ate they had to produce themselves,

▲ **The changing seasons:** life was hard for the peasants who laboured long hours in the manor lands outside the castle walls. Each season brought new kinds of exhausting work, in an endless routine that often led to an early death.

from the pigs, cattle, and geese that grazed on the common land. (This was unfenced pasture – grassland – shared by everyone.) Peasants were sometimes so desperate for food, however, that they were prepared to risk illegal hunting in the forests.

Most people who lived on the land were actually owned by the lord of the manor. Called 'villeins', they were given land by the lord to live on and farm. In return, they had to give some of their crops and animals to the lord as a tax.

Villeins also had to give their labour to their lord. For a certain number of days each year, they worked in the lord's

Beer and Brewing

Making ale was the job of the maltster and brewess. The maltster soaked barley until it sprouted, then roasted it to make malt. This process turned the grain's starch into sugar. Grinding the malt between millstones got it ready for the next process – brewing. The brewess boiled the malt with water, then added yeast. This tiny plant turned the sugar in the malt to alcohol. The strong ale that brewing produced was popular for three reasons. It gave the peasants a lot of the energy they needed. The boiling killed germs, so unlike water (see page 14), ale was safe to drink. And the alcohol helped the peasants forget all the hard work they would have to do the next day!

▶ **Brewing:** this was hard work, and the brewess or ale wife often got more complaints than thanks. Testing her work was the job of the ale-conner, who sat in a pool of ale for half an hour: poor quality ale stuck his trousers to the bench!

fields, growing crops to feed those in the castle. These were called boon days. The reeve, who was in charge of the manor, could call boon days whenever he pleased. For example, there would be boon days called in the spring for ploughing – usually when the weather was perfect for the peasants to plough their own land. And then there would be more boon days in the summer for harvest – again, just when the peasants wanted to reap their own wheat and barley.

The grain the peasants grew went into making bread and ale. To make bread flour, the miller ground the grain between two huge round stones in a mill powered by water or wind (see page 9). Coarse sieves removed some of the bran, but after baking even the whitest bread was heavier and coarser than today's brown loaves.

It's harvest time: the squire helps
  To tie the corn into a bale.
He mops his brow and dreams he has
  A loaf of bread and jug of ale.
But from the castle comes the rival
  With some guards in armour clad.
He points a finger and declares:
  'He stole the plate – arrest the lad!'

18

Crime and Punishment

Castle courts dealt harshly with anyone who broke the law. Minor villains faced shaming public punishments. For more serious offences the penalty might be branding, losing an ear or nose, or even death by hanging.

'Justice' in the Middle Ages often meant 'death'. Execution (punishment killing) was the penalty for all but the most minor crimes. A thief who stole a sheep, for example, risked being hanged by the neck with a rope if he was caught and convicted.

This punishment might seem harsh, but in fact executions were rare. Before a criminal could be hanged, he had to be tried. This meant that a court – a special meeting – decided whether he had done wrong. Sometimes the lord of the castle or his marshall made the decision in the court, but often a jury decided. Juries were groups of ordinary men, sometimes the neighbours of the prisoner. They knew how serious the punishment was,

▲ **The pillory:** this was used to humiliate the criminal, but it could also be dangerous. Unpopular victims might be pelted with so much rubbish that they died. There were some cruel refinements, too: gossips, for example, had their ears nailed to the wood.

and often let people go, rather than see them killed. Courts had the power to give less serious punishments. They sometimes chose to fine villains (make them pay money or possessions) rather than kill them.

Where they could not decide if someone was guilty (had done wrong), courts could order a trial by ordeal. This was a special kind of test in which people believed that God was the judge. Many ordeals involved suffering, and some were a punishment in themselves. For example, in the ordeal of hot iron a prisoner had to either walk barefoot over sheets of

red-hot metal, or carry a lump of hot iron in his or her hand. Prisoners were judged guilty if their wounds did not heal in three days.

Ordeal by water was another way of testing guilt. Here, prisoners were thrown into a pond or river. People believed that water was pure and would not accept the impure, so prisoners who sank escaped further punishment – if they didn't drown first.

Other ordeals weren't as bad. In the ordeal of the cross, two people whose statements disagreed both stood with their arms outstretched during a church service. The one whose arms dropped first was judged to be a liar. (It's not as easy as it sounds – try it for five minutes).

Prisoners who refused to take part in an ordeal were made outlaws. This meant that they had to leave their homes and families and give up all their possessions. An outlaw no longer had the protection of the law, and anyone could kill him: 'It was the right and duty of every man to pursue him, to ravage his land, to burn his

▶ **Hanging:** villains who were executed were sometimes 'hung in chains' on a gibbet (a wooden frame) as a warning to others. The 'chains' were actually a metal cage which prevented the body from being taken down for burial.

house, to hunt him down like a wild beast and to slay him.' Outlawry was also used as a punishment for other serious crimes. Minor criminals who escaped execution, fines, or outlawry could still suffer horrible punishment. Some were branded – they had a mark burned into their skin – or had an ear or their nose cut off. The lucky ones just got a spell in the stocks or pillory. These wooden frames held the prisoner tightly by the hands or legs while passers-by pelted them with mud, stones, dung, or rubbish.

▲ **Ordeal by hot iron:** the terrible burns caused by this ordeal often took weeks to heal, yet prisoners were judged guilty if their wounds had not cleared up within three days.

The squire is tried in the manor court,
    Accused of stealing a golden plate.
The rival's made up a wicked plot –
    He wants the daughter for his mate.
The punishment for theft is death.
    The jury thinks: 'That could be me!
Perhaps he did it – maybe not?'
    They tell the Marshall: 'Set him free.'

Warfare

In story-book battles, noble knights fight bravely in shiny armour, their colourful flags flapping boldly in the wind. But real warfare was different. Muddy, bloody, and deadly, it left battlefields covered with bodies, and devastation in the countryside.

Riding to war was slow, complicated, and expensive. A knight did not fight alone: usually four or five other soldiers followed him into battle on foot, or on cheap, wheezing horses. These foot soldiers wore little armour. They fought with longbows or crossbows, or with long spears. Knights also took with them at least one squire, who did not fight. Instead he worked as a helper: he dressed his master in armour, kept him supplied with weapons, caught his horse if the knight fell from the saddle, and held several horses in reserve in case they were needed.

▲ **The cavalry charge:** riding into battle, knights wore light-weight armour. They used their lowered lances to knock the opposing knights from the saddle.

To support these squires and fighting men, there were craftsmen such as blacksmiths and saddlers. Servants provided some of the comforts of home. There were surgeons to treat wounds and carters to move the luggage – and even washerwomen and musicians to keep the knights clean and entertained. When the enemy was near, all these non-fighting helpers were left behind in the baggage-train, and the knights and foot soldiers prepared themselves to fight.

Battles began with a cavalry charge: the mounted knights (or cavalry) formed lines and galloped towards each other with their lances lowered, just like in stories of chivalry. After this first charge, battles became much more confused. In armies today, generals and other officers organize the fighting and give orders. In the Middle Ages, the knights were all noblemen and

But as the plate still can't be found
  (It seems to have completely vanished),
The Baron cries out: 'You must leave!
  Leave my home – you're hereby banished!'
Far away our hero rides
  Until a knight says, 'Come here, sonny!
You could be a mercenary,
  Fight for me and earn some money.'

▸ **Fighting on foot:** if a knight was knocked from his horse, he was in greater danger, for he no longer towered high over foot soldiers. His battle armour still offered useful protection, but it also slowed him down and made fighting on foot more tiring.

equal to each other, so nobody took control. The result was chaos. Battles broke up into many smaller fights as groups of knights attacked each other with swords, either on horseback or on foot.

The victors in these fights did not try very hard to kill their enemies, for a noble knight was worth money. As a prisoner, he could be ransomed – sold back to his family. Defeated knights were treated well, living more like the guests of their captors than their prisoners.

Foot soldiers were not so lucky. Lightly protected in chain mail and helmet (see page 22), they had few defences against a knight on horseback. Once the

▸ **Capture:** this meant humiliating defeat for a knight. He had escaped death, but his captors were likely to strip him of his valuable armour.

knights on the winning side had captured their noble foes, they often turned on the defeated archers and lancers and killed them without mercy.

Ordinary people also suffered when an army marched through their neighbourhood. Knights could not possibly carry with them enough food for many months of fighting, so they lived off the land. This meant that they simply stole what they needed from the farms and towns they came to. Armies often took every single animal and the seed-corn saved for the following year. With no beasts to breed from and no seed to plant in the spring, the farmers and their families starved.

22

Armour

Like a metal skin that completely covered a knight's body, armour was strong yet light. Clever joints protected even the knees and elbows, and a padded suit beneath the armour plates helped to soften blows.

Warriors everywhere have worn armour to protect themselves against their enemy's weapons. Japanese samurai wore tough bamboo suits; the armour of the Aztecs of Mexico was made of cotton quilted with feathers that was surprisingly tough. European armour in the Middle Ages began as an iron helmet and a very strong coat of scale or mail. Scale armour was made by sewing horn or metal plates to a padded garment. Mail was a coat of wire rings linked in a tight yet bendy mesh.

As time went on, though, knights demanded extra protection against cuts and blows. Armourers responded with a body-covering

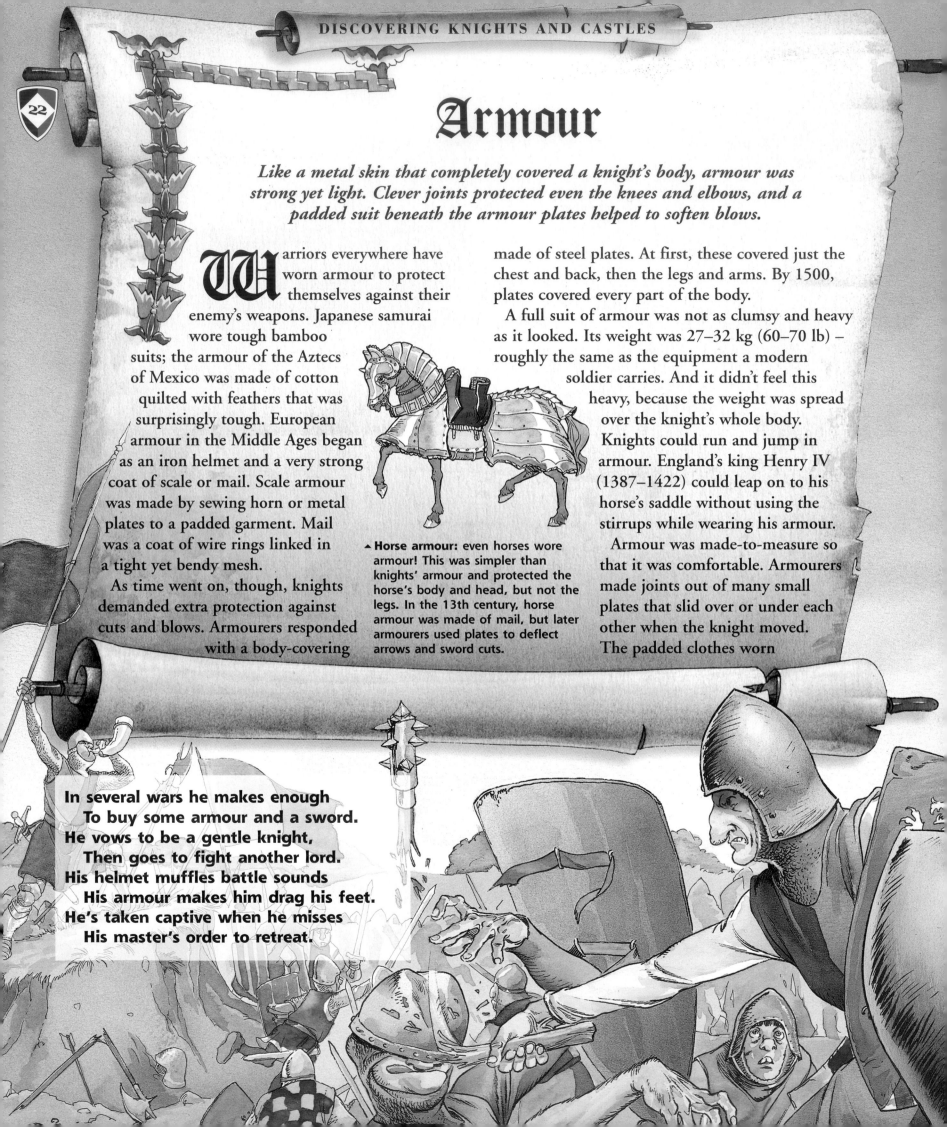

▲ **Horse armour:** even horses wore armour! This was simpler than knights' armour and protected the horse's body and head, but not the legs. In the 13th century, horse armour was made of mail, but later armourers used plates to deflect arrows and sword cuts.

made of steel plates. At first, these covered just the chest and back, then the legs and arms. By 1500, plates covered every part of the body.

A full suit of armour was not as clumsy and heavy as it looked. Its weight was 27–32 kg (60–70 lb) – roughly the same as the equipment a modern soldier carries. And it didn't feel this heavy, because the weight was spread over the knight's whole body. Knights could run and jump in armour. England's king Henry IV (1387–1422) could leap on to his horse's saddle without using the stirrups while wearing his armour.

Armour was made-to-measure so that it was comfortable. Armourers made joints out of many small plates that slid over or under each other when the knight moved. The padded clothes worn

In several wars he makes enough
   To buy some armour and a sword.
He vows to be a gentle knight,
   Then goes to fight another lord.
His helmet muffles battle sounds
   His armour makes him drag his feet.
He's taken captive when he misses
   His master's order to retreat.

1050 **1250** **1350** **1450** **1500**

▲ **Heavyweight:** armour offered European knights increasing protection through the centuries, but safety came at a price. A full suit of plate armour from the 16th century weighed twice as much as a coat of mail from three centuries earlier.

underneath armour stopped the metal from chaffing the skin, but they couldn't prevent bruising or broken bones if a foe scored a direct hit with a sword or mace. The padding also made armour hot. During the Crusades (religious wars in the Middle East) knights dropped dead inside their metal suits from heat-stroke.

The craft skills needed to make armour were not cheap. In the 16th century, a good suit cost a knight about as much as a small car would cost today. Only the rich could afford fashionable designs. On the battlefield, each

knight's armour was different from the next, and most wore a motley collection of some new pieces and others that were very out of date. The richest used the expense of armour to show off their wealth, with chest plates engraved and decorated with gold and silver.

For most knights, strength was more important than appearance. To be sure that they were safe inside their metal suits, knights demanded quality control. Armourers used bows to shoot at the plates, and armour that repelled the arrows was called 'armour of proof'. As weapons became more powerful, proof armour got heavier and heavier. Finally, the introduction of guns in the 16th century made all plates useless. Those that were strong enough to stop a bullet were too heavy to wear.

24

Weapons

Knights went to war with long lances and razor-sharp swords. The foot soldiers who fought alongside them also used swords, or poles with deadly tips. And from the 14th century a new kind of bow – the longbow – transformed warfare.

Lance

This thick wooden pole was as long as a car, and tipped with sharpened iron. A knight held the lance under his arm and used it to knock his opponent from the saddle. He couldn't do this without the help of his horse, which he urged into a fast gallop. At top speed, the weight of the horse and knight gave the lance tremendous power.

Sword

The knight's sword weighed 1.3–1.8 kg (3–4 lb) and was extremely sharp. When swung with great force, it could remove a man's head in a single chop. Knights used swords measuring about 90 cm (36 in) for slashing until

▲ **Pole arms:** there were many types of these, with points, hooks, and axe-blades at the tip. All did the same job – they kept the enemy at a safe distance.

the 14th century, when armour got strong enough to deflect sword blows. Armourers then began to make longer swords with more pointed tips. These were better for stabbing through gaps between armour plates.

Falchion

Foot soldiers' swords, called falchions, were sharpened along only one edge. These were shorter than knight's swords and were made heavier at the tip to increase their cutting power.

Pike

The foot soldier's most common pole arm was the pike, which was a type of overgrown spear. At 6 m (20 ft), it was long enough to keep a mounted knight at a safe distance.

His guards are armed, there's no escape
  Unless a great big ransom's paid.
He writes a letter to his love:
  'Do not forget me, my sweet maid.'
His sweetheart sends him cake to eat –
  A dagger's hidden, baked inside.
He picks the locks, escapes from jail,
  And flees across the countryside.

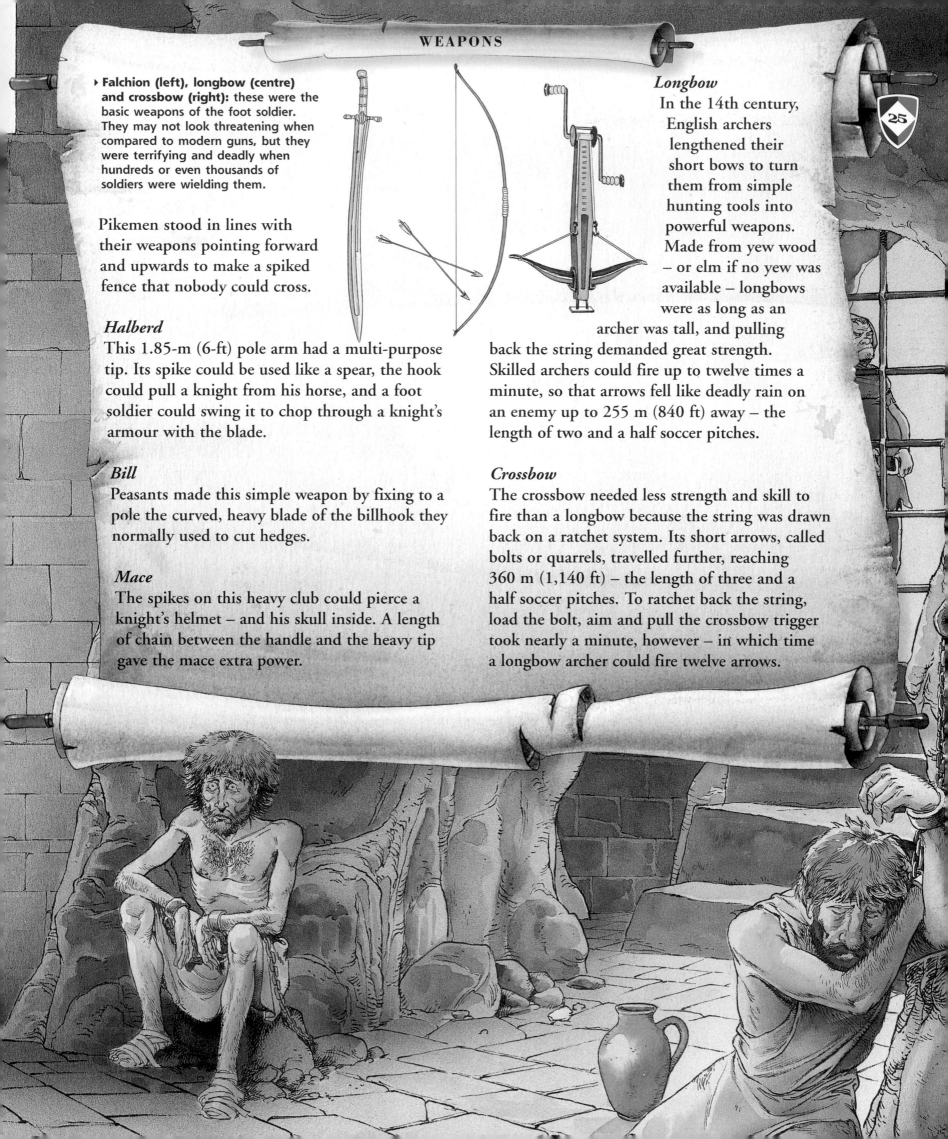

▶ **Falchion (left), longbow (centre) and crossbow (right):** these were the basic weapons of the foot soldier. They may not look threatening when compared to modern guns, but they were terrifying and deadly when hundreds or even thousands of soldiers were wielding them.

Pikemen stood in lines with their weapons pointing forward and upwards to make a spiked fence that nobody could cross.

Halberd
This 1.85-m (6-ft) pole arm had a multi-purpose tip. Its spike could be used like a spear, the hook could pull a knight from his horse, and a foot soldier could swing it to chop through a knight's armour with the blade.

Bill
Peasants made this simple weapon by fixing to a pole the curved, heavy blade of the billhook they normally used to cut hedges.

Mace
The spikes on this heavy club could pierce a knight's helmet – and his skull inside. A length of chain between the handle and the heavy tip gave the mace extra power.

Longbow
In the 14th century, English archers lengthened their short bows to turn them from simple hunting tools into powerful weapons. Made from yew wood – or elm if no yew was available – longbows were as long as an archer was tall, and pulling back the string demanded great strength. Skilled archers could fire up to twelve times a minute, so that arrows fell like deadly rain on an enemy up to 255 m (840 ft) away – the length of two and a half soccer pitches.

Crossbow
The crossbow needed less strength and skill to fire than a longbow because the string was drawn back on a ratchet system. Its short arrows, called bolts or quarrels, travelled further, reaching 360 m (1,140 ft) – the length of three and a half soccer pitches. To ratchet back the string, load the bolt, aim and pull the crossbow trigger took nearly a minute, however – in which time a longbow archer could fire twelve arrows.

Sieges and Siege Engines

Castles were strong enough to resist the arrows and charges of the most powerful armies. Often the only way to capture them was by siege – surrounding the castle and waiting until the defenders starved or surrendered.

By building camps all the way round a castle, attackers hoped to prevent the garrison – the defenders trapped inside – from getting food or supplies. Attackers also tried to stop the defenders' friends and allies from reaching the castle to fight alongside them. If a castle's water supply came from a stream or river, the besieging army might try to divert it. Then thirst would force the garrison to surrender.

When food ran out, people in besieged castles grew desperate. They ate their horses, then dined on whatever else was left, including dogs and rats. At the siege of Calais in 1346, the starving French defenders threw out anyone who could not fight. These sick and injured people were trapped between the two armies. They were so hungry that they even ate babies.

If hunger and thirst didn't make those in the castle surrender, attackers used different tactics. They tried to break down the castle walls, or to climb over them. Miners dug tunnels under the walls to make them collapse. Defenders on the walls above fired a barrage of arrows to prevent this, so miners worked under a moving building called a tortoise or cat. Castle builders took precautions against miners – moats, for example, caused their tunnels to flood.

◄ **Catapults:** weapons like this onager used twisted cords for power. The cords unwound like rubber bands, hurling rocks at the massive walls.

He sees the castle in the distance
　　With noisy soldiers all around it
Firing cross-bows and shouting 'Missed us!'
　　The castle is besieged! Surrounded!
They've seen him! There's nowhere to hide,
　　He mustn't give the game away.
Pretending that he's on their side,
　　He helps to load the trebuchet.

Siege Weapons and Engines

The attackers' movable buildings or siege engines were covered in animal hides soaked in water to provide a defence against flaming arrows fired from the beseiged castle's walls. Their nicknames – such as cat and bear – may have come from these animal-skin covers.

Miners could dig beneath the castle walls protected by the tortoise or cat. Like a real tortoise, this mobile building crept slowly forward as the troops inside advanced.

The battering ram was a whole tree that swung from ropes in a stout frame. Positioned at a castle entrance, it could smash a hole in the wooden gate.

The most powerful siege weapons were those designed to batter down the castle walls. Working like gigantic catapults, they hurled heavy rocks and other missiles. The strongest of all was the trebuchet, a monster as high as a house. It had a huge weight at one end of its long arm, which provided the power to fling a rock heavier than a man more than twice the length of a soccer pitch – over 200 m (660 ft). Trebuchets could also be terror weapons, used to fling the heads of executed prisoners or the rotting bodies of dead animals over castle walls.

▲ **The trebuchet:** loaded with specially-trimmed rocks of equal size, the trebuchet could pound the same spot on a wall over and over again.

◄ **The belfry:** if attackers wanted to scale a castle's wall, they used a belfry or bear, a massive tower on wheels with ladders inside. The belfry protected the attackers from arrows fired by the castle archers.

28

Heraldry

Hidden inside their armour, knights looked alike. To avoid being mistaken for their enemies in battle, they painted patterns on their shields identifying their families. The study and use of these 'arms' was the art of the herald.

Flapping on a brightly-coloured flag, or embroidered on a coat of arms worn over armour, a knight's arms made clear who he was. They also proved he was noble – a member of an important and powerful family. Arms were pictures and not writing, so even people who couldn't read could recognize them.

Arms were like today's supermarket brands – their special arrangement of colours and shapes made them easy to pick out, even at a distance. They started in a simple way, with bold shapes and perhaps strange beasts as family badges. But as more and more people acquired coats of arms, they gradually became more complicated. The earliest coats of arms might have had just a single image or 'device'

on a plain background. Later ones had several different devices and patterned backgrounds.

Coats of arms also became more complicated when knights married. Knights merged their arms with those of their wives, making patterns like chessboards. Heralds – knights' messengers – had the job of devising and describing coats of arms. This art became known as heraldry.

Heralds used the French language to describe or blazon coats of arms. For instance, when a herald said 'argent a lion rampant gules' he meant 'a silver background with a red lion standing up on it'.

Heraldry did not end when knights no longer fought in armour. Families that can trace their ancestors back many centuries still use the colourful shields today, but not in battle. Arms are now used more often for decoration.

Achievement of Arms

A coat of arms with all its supporting elements, such as crest, supporters, and motto, was called an achievement of arms.

Crest: knights fixed personal badges made of wood or leather to the tops of their helmets. They looked like cocks' combs or crests.

Mantling: in hot sun knights protected their heads and shoulders with a slashed cloth, and later painted it on their arms.

Wreath: this circle of twisted silk or cloth held the mantling in place on the helmet.

Crown: only kings and nobles could include a crown on their arms.

Helmet: sitting on top of the shield, the helmet showed how important the knight was. The helmet of a king was gold and faced out. Squires had steel helmets that faced sideways.

Supporters: human or animal figures held up the shield. They may have begun as pictures of the servants in fancy dress who supported the knight's real shield at tournaments.

Shield: the main sign (the charge) on the shield was often a clever joke. Knight Thomas Courbet, for instance, had a crow on his shield, because the French word for a crow, corbeau, sounds like Courbet.

Quartering: a married knight used his wife's arms on half his shield; when his son married, the shield was again divided in two, so the arms soon began to look like chessboards.

Motto: below the shield or above the crest, knights put mottos. These were clever sayings or rules to guide their lives. This motto is in Latin and means 'labour with counsel' – in other words, work sensibly.

LABORE ET CONSILIO

The siege goes on for months and months,
    All the troops have had enough.
Our hero cries 'Make me a herald –
    I'll pretend you're all still tough!'
But in the castle he reveals
    The battle plans of those outside.
So soon the foes are all defeated
    And he's free to claim his bride.

30

Sport and Entertainment

KERRUNCH! With a noisy splintering of lances, a charging knight knocks an opponent from his horse. But this isn't real warfare – it's a joust or tournament, a mock battle in which knights fight to win bets and amuse their friends and families.

Castle life wasn't all work and warfare: there was plenty of fun, too. Some of the games that children played in the Middle Ages are still popular (see page 31), but nothing today quite compares with the grandeur and excitement of a tournament.

These began as 'friendly' battles with real weapons. All too often, though, the competitors took the game too seriously, resulting in injury and death. By the middle of the 14th century, tournaments had become formal contests between pairs of knights. They used blunt, hollowed-out

▲ **Having fun:** bobbing for apples on a tree was as difficult as the modern Christmas game of plucking them from a bowl of water.

lances that broke easily, and they wore special heavyweight armour. These safety precautions reduced deaths, but broken bones were common.

The tournament took place in the lists – a flat patch of land divided in two by a long, low fence called a tilt. The two knights mounted their horses at opposite ends and sides of the tilt, lowered their lances – and charged. Each one aimed to knock his rival from the saddle, without falling from his own horse.

The defeated knight gave up to the victor his expensive armour and horse, and sometimes his liberty, too. Jousting champions could ransom those they defeated (see page 21), and some knights became very rich this way.

There was more to tournaments than fighting. They were fun

The Baron says 'We'll mark the wedding
  With a jolly tournament.'
The rival tries a lively handspring
  To hide his disappointment.
From his shirt falls something shiny –
  The golden plate! So he's the thief!
They march him off for execution
  Sobbing in his handkerchief.

Children's Games

While their parents rode real horses, children had to manage with each other's backs. The game of knights was like a piggyback tournament, with pairs of players taking turns to be horse or rider. The 'knights' pushed and shoved with their shoulders to make their opponents fall.

Toys were simple: children played with kites or with wooden tops that they kept spinning with lengths of dried eel skin. For balloons, they begged animal bladders from butchers and blew them up to float on ponds.

◄ **Hobby-horses:** charging with make-believe horses and blunt lances was a harmless pastime for boys, and taught them valuable skills.

▸ **Battledore and shuttlecock:** this old children's game led to the modern sport of badminton.

events to which the organizer invited friends and relations from all around. Knights set up their colourful tents near the lists, and the most important spectators watched from a raised wooden stand. There was a carnival atmosphere, with minstrels playing, and often feasting and celebrations after the jousting.

When there wasn't a joust planned, knights and their families had plenty of other ways to amuse themselves. Within the castle they played board games like backgammon and chess, and when the weather was fine they went out riding for pleasure, or hawking and hunting (see page 7). Hunts were often grand affairs in which noblemen rode out with packs of hounds to chase deer and wild boar. On a big hunt, they took along dozens of servants, including cooks, scribes, chamberlains, and even the castle chaplain. Castle women hunted, too, catching rabbits with the help of tame ferrets.

▲ **Board games:** chess and backgammon helped to pass the time when it was raining.

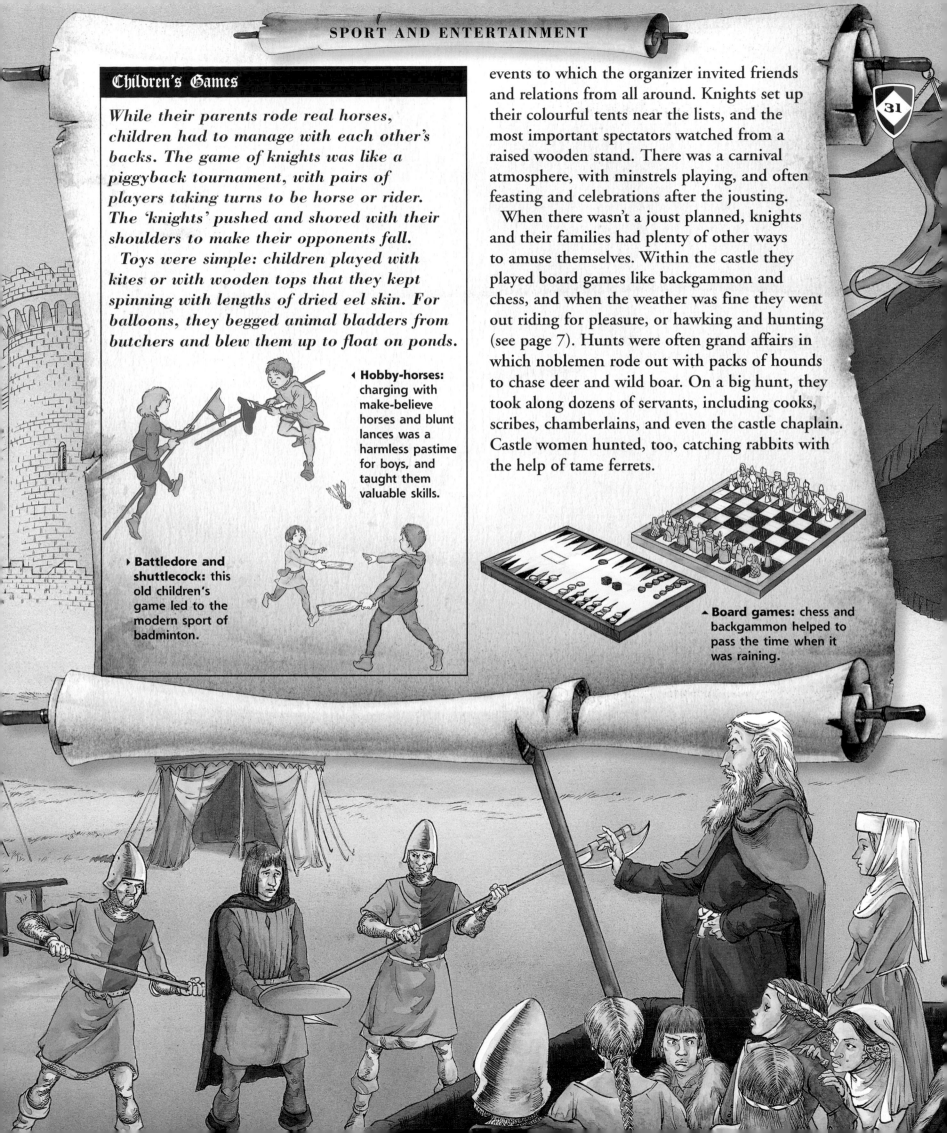

32

Index